CONTENTS

WHO WERE THE MAYA?

Over 2,300 years ago, the Mayan people of Central America and southern Mexico built a remarkable civilisation in the jungle. Their world was divided into many city-states, like small kingdoms, each with its own ruler. At the centre of each was a sacred city. Here the Maya built grand palaces decorated with beautiful carvings and paintings, and pyramids to rival those of ancient Egypt.

Archaeologists believe that this Mayan pyramid at Uxmal was built in five phases, this last one in c. 900 CE. The jungle has grown back over land once cleared for farming.

4

This map shows the main sites of the ancient Maya in Central America. Modern country borders are shown in red.

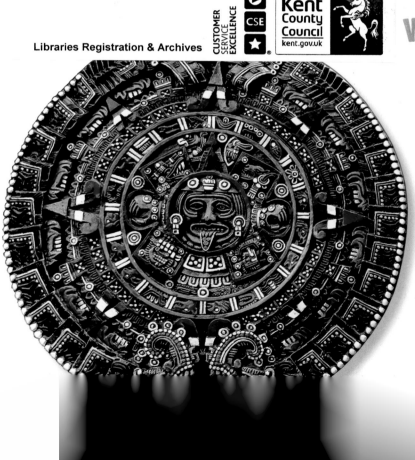

This edition published in 2015 by Franklin Watts

Copyright © Franklin Watts 2015

Franklin Watts
338 Euston Road
London NW1 3BH

Franklin Watts Australia
Level 17/207 Kent Street
Sydney, NSW 2000

Series editor: John C Miles
Editor: Sarah Ridley
Art director: Peter Scoulding
Series designer: John Christopher/White Design
Picture research: Diana Morris

Dewey number: 972

ISBN 978 1 4451 3414 7

Printed in China

Franklin Watts is a division of Hachette Children's Books,
an Hachette UK company.

www.hachette.co.uk

5

Awesome innovations

The ancient Maya were very religious, and much of their world was built around worshipping their gods and goddesses. They made amazing advances in science, mathematics, writing and art. Observatories were built to study the stars and planets, and Mayan mathematicians developed a number system using zero. These helped the Maya work out an accurate calendar. The ancient Maya also had their own system of picture writing, called hieroglyphs, which they carved into stone and inked onto bark paper.

A civilisation disappears

Many Mayan ideas were based on those of the Olmec, a mysterious people who lived around 1200–400 BCE. The height of Mayan civilisation was between 250 BCE and 900 CE — this is referred to as the Classic period. After this, many Mayan cities were abandoned. Recent research suggests that a terrible drought caused the collapse of their civilisation. However, in places Mayan culture continued until the 16th century when Spanish conquerors invaded parts of Central America, and there are still Mayan people living there today.

SOCIETY SNAPSHOT

Within each city-state, society was divided into layers. At the top was the king or queen and the royal family, who were seen to have god-like powers. Below them came nobles and priests, followed by craftspeople and merchants. Farmers and servants were next, with slaves at the very bottom.

Cutting edge

Most normal Mayan families lived in villages surrounding the cities. Their houses were lightly constructed to stay cool in the hot climate of Central America, and had thatched roofs. Sometimes the ancient Maya buried the family's dead under the foundations of the house.

6 Royal benefits

It was easy to tell what class a Maya belonged to — the bigger the headdress, the more important the person! The king often wore jaguar skins and a huge headdress with feathers from the quetzal bird. He lived in luxury at a palace in the city centre, and he was allowed many wives, in order to ensure he had an heir.

This diagram shows the different levels of Mayan society.

THE KING
and royal family ruled the land and were thought to be god-like.

PRIESTS
carried out religious rituals and sacrifices.

NOBLES
owned land and had much wealth and power.

CRAFTSMEN AND MERCHANTS
made and sold crafts and other goods.

FARMERS, SERVANTS AND SLAVES
worked for the upper classes.

A modern reconstuction of a Mayan house, with its thatched roof.

Growing up

Children of noble birth learned writing, maths and religion from educated priests. The children of merchants and craftspeople learnt skills from their parents. So a boy learnt farming or a craft from his father, and a girl helped her mother in the garden, learned to weave and cook, tend the house and care for younger children. Girls as young as 14 and boys aged 18 could be married. An astrologer picked a suitable partner for the young people by comparing their birth charts.

Around the world

c. 3000–30 BCE Egypt
Ancient Egyptian society is made up of many different levels, but men and women from all classes except slaves are equal under the law.

1066–1500s CE Britain
The English ruler owns all the land and gives some of it to powerful barons in return for their loyal support and some money. In the same way, the barons give land to knights, who allow peasants to use strips of land to grow food in return for a share of the harvest and some working hours.

1603–1867 CE Japan
A system called *shinōkōshō* places samurai warriors at the top and merchants at the bottom level of society.

CHOCOLATE GODDESS

The ancient Maya were among the first people to grow cacao, from which chocolate is made. Chocolate was so important that the Maya prayed to a goddess — Ixcacao — to watch over their cacao trees. As well as harvesting fruits and hunting wildlife in the forest, they also grew a range of nutritious crops.

8

Hot chocolate

Roasted cacao beans, water, cornmeal and chilli peppers were mixed together and poured from cup to cup to make a thick, bitter drink with a frothy top. The Maya believed that this bitter chocolate had many health benefits, and today many scientists agree.

This Mayan statuette depicts the Mayan goddess Ixcacao – the goddess of chocolate.

Slash and burn

Mayan farmers cleared land for farming by cutting down jungle plants and burning them. The ash fertilised the crops they planted. They had small farms and mostly grew sweetcorn (maize), beans and squash. Maize made up 75 per cent of their diet. It was used to make tortillas, a flat bread served rolled up with meat or vegetables.

Gardens and hunting

Mayan women kept a kitchen garden, where they grew agave, tomatoes and chilli peppers. In small orchards they grew cacao, avocado and papaya fruit trees. The men hunted for food, bringing home quail, partridge, deer, ducks, crocodiles and even spider monkeys.

Cutting edge

The Maya believed that the body and spirit are closely connected. If someone had a minor illness, they would be given a tea made with medicinal herbs. But if a person was very ill, it was thought that an evil spirit had captured his or her soul. A medicine man (dressed as above) would perform a ritual, chanting over the patient to get rid of the bad spirit. He might prescribe a medicine made from odd ingredients – such as water infused with a bat or toad!

 ## Around the world

1200 BCE India
Ayurvedic healing techniques are developed to aid harmony of the soul, the mind and the physical senses.

700s CE Middle East
Arab traders introduce sugar cane to the Mediterranean, Mesopotamia, Egypt and North Africa.

1500s–1600s Europe
European explorers bring cocoa beans back to Europe. Gradually, the custom of drinking hot chocolate becomes popular among wealthy people.

UNIQUE BEAUTY

The ancient Maya had unusual ideas about beauty and fashion. They wore a wide variety of colourful clothing and jewellery – the higher their rank in society, the more rich and elaborate their clothes and headdresses. And not only did they decorate their skin with paint and tattoos, but they changed their basic features as well.

10

Clothes or not

Up until the age of five, Mayan children went naked. Then boys wore loincloths and girls wore skirts. Both men and women wore loose-fitting clothes made from woven fabric, dyed in bright reds, blues, greens and yellows.

Cutting edge

When a Mayan baby was born, its mother would strap boards to the front and back of the head for a few weeks. As the baby grew, this would flatten the forehead, a look that was desirable (see right). Crossed eyes were also thought a sign of beauty, as were large noses. Some people went so far as to fix clay to their noses to make them look bigger!

This Mayan carved stone head shows the facial characteristics that the Maya considered desirable.

This wall painting from Bonampak dates from 790 CE and shows dazzling Mayan fashion.

Hair, make-up and jewellery

Both men and women wore their hair long, often in ponytails for men or plaits for women. Tattoos may seem like a modern trend, but the Maya got there first! Ornate tattoos were a symbol of bravery — as it was painful to have the ink pricked into the skin. In order to frighten the enemy, Mayan warriors painted their faces black, white and red, and women wore make-up too. Bracelets, necklaces, nose and ear plugs made of jade, shell or serpentine were worn by both sexes, but men usually wore more jewellery then women.

 ## Around the world

c. 900s–1000 China
Wealthy Chinese begin the painful custom of foot-binding to keep girls' feet small.

c. 1300 Asia
Marco Polo reports that the Kayan women of Thailand use heavy neck rings to lengthen their necks artificially.

1800s Europe and North America
Laced corsets are used in Europe and North America to help give women a fashionable shape, with a small waist.

SWEET SOUNDS

Music and dance were enjoyed by all Maya. The little ocarina (below) is one of many instruments they played. It made a high-pitched, bird-like sound rather like a recorder, and was small enough to carry around. The Maya also left behind some of the most breathtakingly beautiful art in the ancient world. Statues, stone carvings, wall hangings and murals are found all across ancient Mayan lands.

12

Sound of music

Ocarinas were made by skilled craftspeople in the shape of animals, birds and humans. People also played lively music on flutes, gourd rattles and pax — a drum made from tortoiseshell — at monthly festivals. During religious ceremonies, hundreds of people would dance together and go into a trance. The dancers wore elaborate masks in the shape of creatures or monsters that were artworks in themselves.

This ocarina was made from clay, painted and baked into pottery.

Working in clay and stone

The Maya were such skilled craftspeople that even everyday pots, vases, cups and plates were works of art. Pottery figures of people, gods, goddesses and animals decorated homes. The city of Copan is renowned for its amazing statues, as well as buildings carved with ornate reliefs and glyphs. The stonework was once painted in bright colours that have faded with time.

13

This Mayan plate dates from c. 600-900 CE. It was used to hold sacred food for feasts and depicts a masked man wearing a jaguar pelt and carrying a spear.

Cutting edge
Some of the most vibrantly coloured murals in the ancient world have been found in a temple at Bonampak (see page 11). They cover three rooms and show scenes from the lives of the ruler who lived there around 800 CE.

Around the world

2000 BCE Greece
The first lyres – U-shaped stringed instruments – are played in the Cyclades on Minoan Crete.

210–209 BCE China
A life-sized terracotta army of 8,000 soldiers is placed in pits near Emperor Qin Shi Huang's mausoleum (tomb).

c. 800–1200 Pacific Islands
Giant statues are built by native Polynesian people on Easter Island.

OLDEST BOOK

The Maya developed a system of writing with symbols that were carved onto stone, or painted on paper made from bark strips. The pages were sewn together to make books, including the vibrant *Dresden Codex* (far right). It is a rich work that has helped archaeologists to discover much about ancient Mayan writing and culture.

14

Some of the Mayan glyphs, or hieroglyphs, are shown here.

Cutting edge

In ancient Mayan writing, a symbol could represent a syllable in a word, then be combined with another symbol to make up a whole word. But single symbols could also express more common words, such as WINIK (person), NAJ (house) and K'AK (fire). To make things even more complicated, just as in English, there were different ways to 'spell' the same word!

WITZ 'mountain'

K'IN 'sun'

B'ALAM 'jaguar'

K'AK 'fire'

JUUN 'book'

JA' 'water'

AJAW 'lord'

MUYAL 'cloud'

K'UK' 'quetzal'

CHAN 'snake'

CH'UL 'holy'

CHOK 'to scatter'

Written in stone

Around 23 languages were spoken in different parts of the ancient Mayan civilisation. However, only one language was written down as glyphs or hieroglyphs, a system of pictures and symbols that stand for words and syllables. These were first carved on stone stelea, monuments to mark special events such as battles, or gravestones to honour people who had died. The oldest example is from c. 300 BCE.

A single page from the *Dresden Codex*, the oldest and best preserved of the four surviving books of the Maya.

Breaking the codex

The *Dresden Codex* is the oldest known book written in ancient Mayan. Its pages are crammed with information important to the Maya: almanacs telling them when to plant crops, predictions about the future, and tables recording the movements of Venus.

When Spanish conquistadors invaded Meso-America in the 16th century, they wanted to rule the Maya and claim their wealth for Spain. In 1562, a Catholic bishop, Diego de Landa, aimed to destroy all the texts of the Maya, so that people would forget their old religion and convert to Christianity. However, four of these amazing books survive today.

15

 ## Around the world

c. 1600–1000 BCE China
During the Shang Dynasty, 'oracle bone' script is etched onto bone or tortoiseshell.

c. 300 BCE Middle East
In Sumer, wedge-shaped cuneiform script is pressed onto wet clay tablets, then left to harden as a permanent 'page'.

196 BCE Egypt
The Rosetta Stone is carved using three scripts: Egyptian hieroglyphs, demotic and Greek. This makes it possible to work out the meaning of all three.

GAME OF THROWS

The Maya were the first civilisation to develop a team sport around 3,500 years ago, in the so-called Preclassic period. Each city-state had at least one giant open-air ball court. Here, a game called pok-a-tok was played – similar to basketball or volleyball. The playing was fast and dangerous, and was taken very seriously.

The largest ball court ever discovered is at Chichen Itza. Built in around 800 CE, it is 175 metres long by 70 metres wide and has 7-metre-high walls along each side.

16

Cutting edge

The Maya were first to play a team sport, probably because they were the first to invent a bouncy rubber ball to play it with! They made the rubber from the sap of the rubber tree. Around 1600 BCE, the Maya discovered how to tap the tree trunk to extract the milky sap. They then mixed it with juice from the Morning Glory vine, and moulded it into balls that weighed up to 3.5 kilograms each.

Holy court

Sacred to the Maya, the game pok-a-tok was a complex ritual. It was based on the Mayan creation story of the Hero Twins, whose ball games disturbed the gods of the underworld, after which the twins had to play to save their lives. The pok-a-tok ball court was made of stone, often painted with bright colours. Players had to send a heavy rubber ball through a high, large stone ring using their hips, knees and arms.

Winner takes all

As with today's football games, crowds of people — men, women and children — would come out to cheer for their favourite players. Sometimes the game was played for fun. But sometimes games were substituted for a war with an enemy city-state. In this case, the losing team might be sacrificed to the gods!

People continue to tap rubber trees today. A worker makes a cut in the bark and collects the sap, called latex, that flows from it.

17

Around the world

Before 776 BCE Greece
First record of running races being held every four years in Olympia, Greece. These are probably the very first Olympic Games.

618 BCE China
Polo is played by both noble men and women of the Tang Dynasty. On one occasion, Emperor Xizong gives a royal military position to the best player.

1100s CE Europe
Tennis begins as a French game called *Paume* (Palm), where players hit the ball over a net with their hands. The racket is invented in the 1300s.

A MAYAN TIME MACHINE

The Mayan civilisation developed a highly accurate and complex system of calendars. Skilled astronomers calculated the movements of the Sun, Moon, planets and constellations, to keep time and to predict the future. Images of calendars are very common in Mayan artefacts. In fact, experts believe that the Maya were obsessed with time.

18

Three calendars

In Mayan timekeeping, three main dating calendars are used together: the Long Count, the Tzolkin (divine calendar) and the Haab (civil calendar). The Long Count calendar is based on 20-day 'months' called uinals, and 18 uinals make up a 'year', or tun, of approximately 360 days. The Tzolkin calendar has a combination of two 'week' lengths: one with 13 numbered days and one with 20 named days. Each day has 'good luck' or 'bad luck' connotations. The Haab is the only calendar that relates to the length of our year, 365 days. Each month has 20 days with separate names like 'Pop' and 'Yax'.

End of the world?
Some people believed that the world would come to an end on 21 December 2012, the day the Mayan calendar supposedly ends. They were afraid a global disaster, such as a comet striking Earth, would destroy all life here. Throughout 2012, US space agency NASA was flooded with phone calls and emails from distressed people. Scientists reassured them there was no catastrophe looming in the skies.

The Tzolkin wheel calendar combines 20 day names with thirteen numbers to produce 260 unique days. It was used to determine religious and ceremonial events and to predict the future.

Ancient time

Modern astronomers think that the Mayan Long Count Calendar is the most complex calendar ever developed by humans. Dates and times carved onto Mayan ruins stretch back a billion billion times further than the Big Bang, which scientists believe happened 13.7 billion years ago.

19

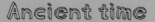

Around the world

36 BCE Central America
First record of Mayan kings using the Long Count Calendar. The knowledge of how to mark time ensures that kings remain powerful.

c. 2400 BCE Britain
Huge stones are raised in a circle at Stonehenge. Some scientists believe that the entire site functioned as an astronomical observatory and a way of marking the passage of time and predicting the summer and winter solstices.

1504 BCE Egypt
The world's oldest-known water clock is buried in the tomb of Pharaoh Amenhotep I (1525–1504 BCE).

STARGAZERS' OBSERVATORY

Astronomy was at the heart of the ancient Mayan world. The Maya believed that by studying the Sun, Moon, planets and stars, they would understand the will of the gods. This dome — El Caracol — was an astronomical observatory where Mayan astronomers charted the skies.

20

Constructed between 600–800 CE, El Caracol at Chichen Itza is an observatory built to line up with the movements of the planet Venus as it crosses the sky.

Cutting edge

Because Venus is so bright in the sky at sunrise or at sunset, the Maya believed it had special significance. Rulers used its 584-day cycle to create a precise calendar – which noted times that the 'the Morning Star' or 'the Evening Star' rose and set – to plan the start of special events, such as wars or the coronation of kings. The Maya also tracked the paths of Mars, Jupiter and Mercury.

Heavenly bodies

Although they did not have telescopes, Mayan astronomers recorded the movements of the heavens with amazing accuracy. They used the square windows in El Caracol to observe the skies, and these were also built to align with the Sun and Venus at certain times of year. The Sun was the most important star as it lit up Earth and made crops grow. The Maya worshipped the sun god Kinich Ahau, who they believed to be joined to the Sun itself.

Number system

Outstanding mathematicians, the ancient Maya developed a number system using 20 instead of 10. They also discovered the concept of zero 1,000 years before European cultures did. To record numbers, the Mayan system used only three symbols: a dot for one, a bar for five, and a seashell for zero. This system allowed the Maya to record important dates and to create their complex calendar.

This stone carving shows the Mayan number system with dots, bars and images.

Around the world

c. 3200 BCE Ireland
The Passage Tomb at Newgrange is built. At the winter solstice (21–22 December), the Sun shines directly into a window to light up the chamber.

928 CE Persia
The first known astrolabe (an instrument that measures the skies) is constructed by Mohammad al-Fazari, an Islamic astronomer and mathematician.

1608 The Netherlands
A Dutch eyeglass maker called Hans Lippershey invents the refracting telescope, which begins a revolution in astronomy.

FANTASTIC CITIES

The ancient Maya built some of the most spectacular cities in ancient history. With a population of between 60,000 and 200,000 people, Tikal was one of the largest cities in the Mayan world. Palaces, pyramids, temples, plazas and streets were carefully planned by skilled architects and constructed from stone by strong labourers. Tikal's ruins are in the modern-day country of Guatemala.

Mystery in the jungle

The city-state of Tikal was at its most powerful between 300 CE and 900 CE. After this time, warfare or drought led to the ancient Maya abandoning the area. Then around 900 CE warfare or drought made the ancient Maya abandon the area, and vines and vegetation swamped the structures. But through the centuries, legends told of a great city in the jungle. In 1956, archaeologists worked through the undergrowth to uncover 3,000 buildings. They also found stelae carved with inscriptions that explain important events in Mayan history.

Sky-high temples

Ancient Mayan step pyramids are an amazing feat of design. Constructed by hand without the help of machines, they had steep steps rising high into the sky, carved with elaborate gods and mystical creatures. A flat base at the top gave Mayan priests a platform to perform ceremonies to honour the gods, while masses of people watched from below.

The city-state of Tikal lasted for about 1,100 years, from 200 BCE to 900 CE. It was a busy trading centre.

Cutting edge

Some archaeologists believe that the staircase of Kulkulcan at Chichen Itza (c. 600 CE) was designed to give off a chirping echo when people clap their hands at its base. This is thought to mimic the chirp of the quetzal – a bird sacred to the Maya – in the jungle.

 ## Around the world

2584 BCE Egypt
Construction begins on the Great Pyramid of Giza. It is the largest pyramid ever built.

c. 200–250 CE Central America
Building ends on the Pyramids of the Sun and Moon in central Mexico by a mysterious people - the Teotihuacanos - who lived at the same time as the Maya, and interacted with them.

c. 1100s Cambodia
The beautifully decorated temple of Angkor Wat is built in the ancient Khmer capital city of Angkor.

AN AQUEDUCT

Every city must have a plentiful source of fresh water for drinking, washing and bathing. At the site of the Mayan city of Palenque, water was everywhere. The problem was, how to tame the many rivers, streams and springs that criss-crossed the land.

24

Moving water

Palenque's King Pakal and his engineers came up with a brilliant solution: they built a system of aqueducts, covered stone channels that guided over 50 kilometres of natural springs, rivers and streams to places where water was needed. This cleared the land making way for the hundreds of buildings to be built, and channelled an amazing 4 million litres of water a day around houses, palaces and temples.

Cutting edge

Mayan aqueducts and buildings were huge feats of engineering. Materials had to be carried to sites by labourers – the Maya did not use the wheel, and so did not have carts for transport. For building, they used chisels, scrapers and other tools made of stone such as flint. They had no metal tools as metal was scarce in the area.

Mayan workers used simple stone tools such as these.

This aqueduct at Palenque was built c. 615–683 CE. It supplied water to the city.

Sunken cenotes

In other Mayan cities, there was no natural water supply. One Mayan solution in the Yucatan peninsula was to use sinkholes or cenotes in the limestone as reservoirs for fresh drinking water. Some occurred naturally, others were created by excavating underground spaces and channelling rainwater into them.

 Around the world

1900 BCE Greece and the Middle East
The first aqueducts in the world are constructed on Minoan Crete and in Mesopotamia.

200 BCE Greece
The ancient city of Pergamon gets its water supply from a sophisticated system of aqueducts.

50 CE France
The largest Roman aqueduct is completed at Pont du Gard in France. It is 49 metres high.

VISIONS OF HEAVEN

For the Maya, death was seen as a continuation of life. The dead person — especially an important leader — was buried with belongings for their journey in the afterlife. This could include food, pottery, slaves and prized possessions, such as a beautiful jade death mask and necklace found in the tomb of King Pakal, who ruled Palenque from 615–683 CE.

26

Spirit levels

The ancient Maya believed that all living things, from trees and plants to animals and humans, have a spirit. Even non-living rocks and objects were thought to have an invisible power. Praying to over 150 gods and goddesses who controlled the Sun, the harvest, rain and the North Star, for instance, the Maya would ask the gods for help with many decisions.

This amazing jade death mask of King Pakal.

A painted vase c. 800 CE shows the Hero Twins of the *Popol Vuh*.

Creation story

The creation story of the Quiché Maya was written down in a book called the *Popol Vuh* (Book of the People). This book tells of the first animals and humans, who were made by the creator Heart of Heaven. It tells of a great flood on Earth, and recounts the adventures of the Hero Twins Hunahpú and Xbalanqué, who play an epic ball game to save their lives. The *Popol Vuh* was recorded in the 18th century by the Spanish priest Francisco Ximénez.

Blood sacrifice

To offer their good intentions to the gods, the Maya carried out bloodletting – cutting into the body or pricking the tongue with a stingray spine, then catching the blood in a bowl. This ritual was often performed by kings or queens, as they were thought to have a direct link to the gods. When there was a drought or famine, a human life might be offered.

Around the world

c. 2600 BCE Middle East
In Sumer, Queen Puabi is buried in a stone tomb, surrounded by gold jewellery, gem-encrusted lyres – and 52 servants.

c. 1323 BCE Egypt
The 19-year-old Pharaoh Tutankhamun dies. His mummy is laid to rest in a gold sarcophagus in the Valley of the Kings.

116 BCE China
Liu Zhu, sixth King of Chu, is buried in Guishan in a tomb filled with jade jewellery, furniture, tools, weapons and even toilets.

TEMPLE OF WARRIORS

The Maya often fought with neighbouring city-states for power and land. A carving on the Temple of the Warriors in Chichen Itza shows fierce Mayan warriors battling with lances. Prisoners of war were taken by the winning side, and often ended up as sacrifices to the gods. The Spanish arrived in Meso-America in 1517, and this marked the start of a fight the ancient Maya, and their neighbours the Aztecs, could not win.

28

Decline

When Spanish invaders arrived on Mayan territory, they brought European diseases such as smallpox, flu and measles. Many Maya died from this 'germ warfare'. By the 1540s, the Spanish controlled most Mayan lands, forcing the people to convert to Christianity. The ancient Mayan civilisation may have ended, but the Maya live on. Today, there are 6 million Mayan people who carry on many traditions from a great civilisation.

Maya warriors painted their bodies in a way similar to this modern re-enactor.

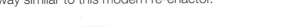

Rival superpowers

Fighting was common between ancient Mayan city-states. In the 6th and 7th centuries, the people of Tikal fought with the people of Calakmul in a series of wars lasting 130 years. This struggle was recorded in glyphs inscribed in stone at Tikal. Smaller local cities, such as nearby Dos Pilas, were used as pawns in the superpowers' game. The record of one battle reads: "Blood flowed, and skulls of the 13 peoples of the Tikal place were piled up."

Keeping the peace

Rulers from a powerful Mayan city-state, Yaxchilan – nicknamed 'the Jaguar Kingdom' – married princesses from rival cities to form alliances between two kingdoms. A Yaxchilan king called Shield Jaguar the Great (681–742) married his first wife, Lady K'abal Xook. But to keep peace with a rival city-state, he also married Lady Eveningstar from Calakmul. Shield Jaguar the Great died at the age of 95 after a 60-year-long reign.

29

This carving features a fierce warrior holding a severed head, from the Temple of the Warriors at Chichen Itza, c.10th century CE.

Around the world

206 BCE China
The Qin Empire collapses after Emperor Shi Huangti dies, leading to a civil war.

60 CE Britain
Queen Boudica leads the Iceni in a successful rebellion against the Romans, but is later defeated.

646 CE Egypt
Egypt is conquered by Arab Muslims under the leadership of Caliph Umar.

GLOSSARY

almanac A calendar made up of important dates and information for the year ahead.

aqueduct A manmade channel that brings water to where it is needed.

archaeologist A person who studies human history through places and objects left behind.

architect Someone who designs buildings.

astrology The study of the movements of the stars and planets and how they might affect people.

astronomy The science of looking at the Sun, Moon, planets and groups of stars.

birth chart A map of where the planets are when a person is born, which astrologers use to try and work out someone's personality.

cacao The seeds (beans) of the cacao tree, which are dried, roasted and ground to make cocoa and chocolate.

cenote An underground reservoir that occurs naturally in the limestone of Yucatan, Mexico.

city-state A city and its surrounding villages and land, ruled by one leader.

conquistadors Groups of Spanish conquerors who invaded Mexico and Peru in the 1500s.

engineer Someone who designs and builds structures or machines.

glyph A character or symbol used to mean a word.

hieroglyph A simplified picture of an object, meant to stand for a word or syllable.

logogram A sign that stands for a word or phrase in writing.

medicine man A healer who is believed to have magic powers to cure a person of disease.

ocarina A small musical instrument with finger holes that makes a flute-like sound.

pok-a-tok The ball game played by the ancient Maya. It was the first-ever team sport.

quetzal A tropical bird that has shiny green and red feathers. It was sacred to the Maya.

staple A food that makes up an important part of the diet, such as bread or maize (sweetcorn).

stela (plural: stelae) A stone column carved with glyphs to mark an important event or a death.

thatched When a roof is made from straw or palm leaves to keep out rain and wind.

trance A dream-like state that people sometimes go into when praying, dancing or meditating.

30

WEBSITES

http://www.mayankids.com/
Learn all about the people, the culture, the gods and goddesses of the Maya, plus the latest news on archaeological finds.

http://www.history.com/topics/maya/videos#the-mayans
Watch a video about the top inventions and achievements of the Maya. Plus videos about Mayan pyramids, palaces and aqueducts.

http://mayas.mrdonn.org/
All about Mayan religion, sport, music, dance, daily life and more. Includes fun Mayan clip art.

http://www.ballgame.org
Learn fascinating facts about the Mayan ball game, watch a recreation of the game, explore what team players wore, and more!

Note to parents and teachers
Every effort has been made by the Publishers to ensure that the web sites in this book are suitable for children, that they are of the highest educational value, and that they contain no inappropriate or offensive material. However, because of the nature of the Internet, it is impossible to guarantee that the contents of these sites will not be altered. We strongly advise that Internet access is supervised by a responsible adult.

TIMELINE

21,000 BCE Hunter-gatherers settle in areas that will become the homelands of the Maya.

3114 BCE According to Mayan mythology, the world is created on a midsummer's day. This is the first day of the Long Count Calendar.

1500 BCE The ancient Maya begin to settle in villages and practise farming.

600 BCE The Maya start digging irrigation canals in order to water their crops.

400 BCE Solar calendars (based on the Sun's cycles) are first used by the Maya.

300 BCE The Maya begin to record language, carving hieroglyphs on stone stelae.

250 CE – 900 CE The ancient Maya begin to build large cities, and develop astronomy and maths, writing and the arts. Rulers are selected to govern the cities.

613–683 CE Pakal the Great rules Palenque and builds palaces, temples and aqueducts.

751 CE Mayan city-states begin to quarrel with each other over land and money.

869 CE The city of Tikal reaches the peak of its popularity, then begins a 30-year decline.

900–1000 CE In the Yucatan Peninsula, Mayan cities start to be abandoned.

1517 Spanish conquistadors arrive in the Yucatan, with Hernan Cortes exploring the area in 1519. This marks the beginning of the end of the civilisation of the ancient Maya.

1562 Bishop Diego de Landa destroys Mayan artefacts and books.

INDEX